WHAT'S IT REALLY LIKE TO BE A
DOCTOR?

CHRISTINE HONDERS

PowerKiDS
press™

New York

T0004885

Published in 2020 by The Rosen Publishing Group, Inc.
29 East 21st Street, New York, NY 10010

First Edition

Editor: Greg Roza
Book Design: Michael Flynn

Photo Credits: Cover, p. 1 Hero Images/Getty Images; pp. 4, 6, 8, 10, 12, 14, 16, 18, 20, 22 (background) Apostrophe/Shutterstock.com; p. 5 FatCamera/E+/Getty Images; p. 7 (boy)TheVisualsYouNeed/Shutterstock.com; pp. 7 (girl), 11, 19, 21 wavebreakmedia/Shutterstock.com; p. 9 Stock Montage/Archive Photos/Getty Images; p. 13 megaflopp/Shutterstock.com; p. 15 antoniodiaz/Shutterstock.com; p. 17 Matej Kastelic/Shutterstock.com; p. 22 Sashkin/Shutterstock.com.

Cataloging-in-Publication Data

Names: Honders, Christine.
Title: What's it really like to be a doctor? / Christine Honders.
Description: New York : PowerKids Press, 2020. | Series: Jobs kids want | Includes glossary and index.
Identifiers: ISBN 9781538349809 (pbk.) | ISBN 9781538349823 (library bound) | ISBN 9781538349816 (6 pack)
Subjects: LCSH: Physicians–Juvenile literature. | Physicians–Vocational guidance–Juvenile literature. | Medicine–Vocational guidance–Juvenile literature.
Classification: LCC R690.H66 2020 | DDC 610.69'5–dc23

Manufactured in the United States of America

CPSIA Compliance Information: Batch #CSPK19. For Further Information contact Rosen Publishing, New York, New York at 1-800-237-9932.

CONTENTS

Is There a Doctor in the House?

Everyone has gone to see the doctor. We go if we aren't feeling well or if we hurt ourselves. Sometimes we go just to make sure we're OK. Doctors don't just take care of sick people. They keep people healthy.

What Doctors Do

Doctors are trained to know what causes **illnesses**. They know how to **treat** sick people and make them feel better. Doctors also know how to keep people from getting sick. They remind people to eat healthy foods and to get the right amount of exercise.

An Early Doctor

Hippocrates (hih-PAH-kruh-tees) was a Greek doctor who lived hundreds of years ago. He taught people that illnesses had natural causes that could be treated by science. Many doctors studied his words. Today, he is remembered as the "father of **medicine**."

Where Doctors Work

Many doctors work in offices. People go to a doctor's office when they don't feel well or for a check-up. Serious **injuries** and illnesses are treated by a doctor in a hospital. Some doctors work in **labs**. They study why people get sick.

A Doctor's Day

Doctors spend most of their time with **patients**. They ask questions about their health and write down the answers. Doctors sometimes test patients' blood. They read the tests and figure out what's wrong. Doctors give patients medicine to make them feel better.

Different Kinds of Doctors

There are many different kinds of doctors. There are doctors for kids and doctors for older people. There are doctors for every part of the body, such as the brain, heart, and skin. Surgeons treat patients by working on their bodies with special tools.

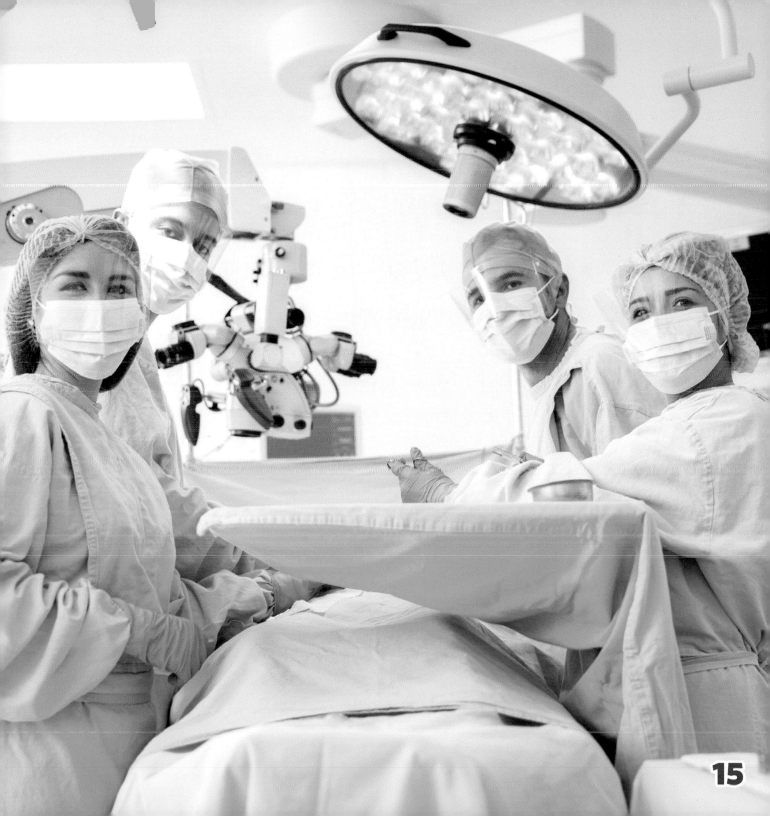

Scientists and Teachers

Some doctors don't see patients. They work in labs making new medicines. They try to cure illnesses like cancer. Some doctors teach students how to become doctors. In a way, most doctors are like teachers. They teach us about our bodies and about living healthy.

How Can I Become a Doctor?

People who want to be doctors go to college. They take many science classes. Then they go to medical school for three to four years. Then, new doctors are trained by older doctors for three to seven more years. Most training takes place in a hospital.

A Doctor's Work Is Hard Work

It's hard to see people hurting every day. It's also **stressful**. Some doctors have to make quick decisions to save someone's life. Doctors get up early and work until late at night. They don't often have a lot of time to spend with their families.

A Job with Rewards

The best part of being a doctor is helping people. Doctors save lives and cure illnesses. But doctors also want people to keep themselves healthy. They want us to feel better and stay better. This makes the hard work worth it!

GLOSSARY

illness: Sickness.

injury: An act that damages or hurts.

lab: A place where tests and experiments are done. Short for "laboratory."

medicine: The science of dealing with the avoiding, cure, or relief of illnesses. Also, a drug someone takes to make them feel better.

patient: A person under the care of a doctor.

stressful: Tending to cause worry or uneasiness.

treat: To give medical care to someone.

INDEX

WEBSITES

Due to the changing nature of Internet links, PowerKids Press has developed an online list of websites related to the subject of this book. This site is updated regularly. Please use this link to access the list: www.powerkidslinks.com/JKW/doctor